Funk Therapy

| Funky | Trendy | Cool | Hip |

Wear The Music You Love!

Visit our merchandise store on our website:

WWW.FUNKTHERAPYMUSIC.COM

10% Discount code: STAYFUNKY

- Hoodies
- Crop Top
- Sweat Pants
- Bucket Hats
- Slides
- Mugs

UNISEX T-SHIRTS

Brown T-Shirt

GRAB IT NOW

Orange T-Shirt

GRAB IT NOW

Beige T-Shirts

GRAB IT NOW

Join our community
@funktherapy2

Pump it up Magazine

TABLE OF CONTENTS

Pump it up
MAGAZINE

PUMP IT UP MAGAZINE —————

LINKS

WEBSITE
www.pumpitupmagazine.com

FACEBOOK
www.facebook.com/pumpitupmagazine

TWITTER
www.twitter.com/pumpitupmag

SOUNDCLOUD
www.soundcloud.com/pumpitupmagazine

INSTAGRAM
pumpitupmagazine

PINTEREST
www.pinterest.com/pumpitupmagazine

PUMP IT UP MAGAZINE
30721 Russell Ranch Road
Suite 140
Westlake Village,
California 91362
United States

📞 **(818)514 – 0038(Ext:102)**
✉ **info@pumpitupmagazine.com**

Greetings Readers,

It's warming up everywhere and the scent of summer is in the air!

The world is changing right before our very eyes. A new normal is upon us .
We just hear of the challenges we are facing on a daily basis.
We pray for the families of those lost in the senseless mass shootings around the US
and the world.
Let us be vigilant and careful and watch our for each other in this day and time.

Summer is coming and we love to have that beach body but we must not get forge
to take care of our mind!

National PTSD Awareness Day is celebrated annually on June 27, It aims to raise
awareness of post traumatic stress disorder.
Narcissistic Abuse can lead to the development of Complex PTSD when living with
unprocessed trauma.
We help you raise awareness by identifying Signs of Narcissistic Abuse Syndrome &
How to Heal From C-PTSD.
We hope that Pump It Up Magazine can contribute to that.

On the cover we have saxophonist Kenny Nigthingale who has played saxophone
since he was 8 years old!
He is currently riding high on the smooth jazz charts around the nation and
continues to inspire the jazz purist with his sultry and gospel tinged songs.

Bassist Mitchell Coleman Jr. and his producer Michael B Sutton has formed a new
sound called Funk Therapy.
The introductory single is a hip hop urban remix of the group Pleasure gem " Giide'
A positive upbeat track on how to glide through each day in the midst of adversity

May God bless you!

Remember , the answer to a linear life is to become creative!

Anissa Sutton

CONTRIBUTORS

EDITOR IN CHIEF
Anissa Sutton

MUSIC
Michael B. Sutton
A. Scott Galloway

MARKETING
Grace Rose

PARTNERS

Editions L.A.
www.editions-la.com

The Sound Of L.A.
www.thesoundofla.com

Info Music
www.infomusic.fr

Delit Face
www.DelitFace.com

L.A. Unlimited
www.launlimitedinc.com

Saxophonist Extraordinaire KENNY NIGHTINGALE

KennyNightingale.com

KENNY NIGHTINGALE DISPLAYS A SPECTACULAR PERFORMANCE ON HIS LATEST SINGLE TITLED "MY SAXOPHONE"

Famously known for his passion and the dedication he puts into all his performances; Kenny Nightingale has continued to extend his uniqueness with his latest release dubbed "My Saxophone".

The saxophone is about the most versatile instrument in the range of timbres. For Nightingale, this is an instrument through which he replicates his own self and how he feels deep within. On his latest project released in May (2022), the prodigy displayed his ingenuity with an awe-inspiring track that will make your ears drop to the soothing sound of his saxophone.
With a chart-topping performance, Kenny Nightingale went all in to evoke a sense of belonging in many smooth jazz enthusiasts.
His single came off with a unique blend of the beloved rhythm and blues captured in a jazz spectrum.

Being a saxophonist based in the US, Nightingale has brought the perception of a saxophone closer in an age drowning in a wide scope of genres. He refers to the saxophone as his favorite instrument among all other instruments on his belt. It was quite expected of him to serve us with this number. Beautifully produced to perfection, "My Saxophone" is an empowering piece that will turn your mood around. Its resonating tones are tuned to the sound that will ramp up your energy and make you fall in love with jazz in general. This is a song written with ultimate precision.

Kenny Nightingale has for quite some time proved to be one of the best artists in his niche. He has been nominated for several awards whilst part of his discography has topped charts such as; The Smooth Jazz 100 Billboard chart & The Smooth Jazz network charts.
Check out his latest single "My Saxophone" on all music platforms and feel the power that lies within.

Website: www.kennynightingale.com
YouTube: https://youtu.be/-3e_imAYctw
Facebook: @Kennyjazzgrooves
Instagram: @Kenny.nightingale
Twitter: @Kennygroove

1. GREAT TO HAVE YOU ON PUMP IT UP MAGAZINE! PLEASE TELL US ABOUT YOUR BACKGROUND.

Kenny Nightingale
My name is Kenny Nightingale and I'm an American based smooth jazz r&b recording artist. I'm originally from the west side of the Motherland Lagos Nigeria Africa. I play music that comes from the deep, and that alone has confirmed to me that playing angelical sounds with a unique blend from all parts of the world is what I'm commissioned to do this day.

2. HOW DID YOU GET STARTED IN THE MUSIC BUSINESS?

Kenny Nightingale
I started playing music at the age of 8 years old. My father is a musician himself. He took my hands along when he saw my interest in the craft, he thought me how to play the Saxophone & percussion.

3. TELL US WHAT'S THE STORY BEHIND YOUR NEW SINGLE "MY SAXOPHONE"

Kenny Nightingale
My Saxophone was inspired by the very instrument itself that I play. It is my favorite among other instruments on my belt. I enjoy playing the saxophone, and why not write something about it I said to myself. And here comes the birth of My Saxophone.

4. WHAT MAKES YOUR PRODUCTIONS UNIQUE? AND HOW WOULD YOU DESCRIBE IT?

Kenny Nightingale
I believe I can safely say that my production is unique in a way that I try to make my music a replication of myself on how I'm feeling deep within when I write and create. I grab ideas from as far as the Motherland to the western world just to create a groove with a unique sound that is different from the others. In this way my music can be categories as jazz, smooth jazz, world beats, rhythm and blues.

" I wanna blow my Saxophone-No, I wanna blow my Saxophone-No. There's no other greater than you, I wanna blow my Saxophone-No. "

5. WHO ARE YOUR BIGGEST MUSICAL INFLUENCES? AND ANY PARTICULAR ARTIST/BAND YOU WOULD LIKE TO COLLABORATE WITH IN THE FUTURE?

Kenny Nightingale
ome of my musical influences are Grover Washington Jr., Jonathan Butler, Slash, John Coltrane, Kenny G, Jimmy Hendricks & Dave Koz just to name a few among others.

6. WHICH IS THE BEST MOMENT IN YOUR MUSICAL CAREER THAT YOU'RE MOST PROUD OF?

Kenny Nightingale
I'm very proud of the way things are going in the right direction for my music. One of my best moment was when I got a call in 2016 that one of my tracks "Gospel Got Jazz" was nominated for The Gospel Choice Awards for best Instrumental. I was very humbled and proud of that project because I couldn't afford to pay for an hotel room when I landed in Oklahoma City from the airport to the studio to finalize my mixing and mastering of that track Gospel Got Jazz. I had to stay up awake all night till the next morning for studio time. Today when I look back intime, I am gracious for brighter days ahead.

I'm also proud of my first major smooth jazz radio single titled Coltrane To Montgomery" that came out in 2020.
It was a smash hit on the smoothjazz.com chart at #24 on the top 100. And it made at #11 on the smooth jazz network billboard charts. I'm so looking forward to the road ahead with this new single and beyond.

7. IF YOU HAD ONE MESSAGE TO GIVE TO YOUR FANS, WHAT WOULD IT BE?

Kenny Nightingale
My message to fans out there is to never give up on you even when everyone has. Keep your head up and stay focused on your goals. For at the appointed time it will surely come to pass as long as you believe.

8. WHAT'S NEXT FOR YOU? ANY UPCOMING PROJECTS OR TOURS?

Kenny Nightingale
The next step for me now is working on getting with an agency that will put Kenny Nightingale on the road. In that way I can see and meetup with my fans out there! And of course I've got the next single project on the way for October of 2022. I'm not going to say what the title is right now, but stay with me on my journey to the promised land and we will celebrate along the way together to this beautiful place called music.

"I would love to collaborate in the near future with artist as Kenny G, Aaron Neville, Jonathan Kenneth Butler and guitarist Slash."

Saxophonist Extraordinaire
KENNY NIGHTINGALE

WWW.KENNYNIGHTINGALE.COM

42 STREAMS OF MUSIC INCOME

If you're a musician or composer, you probably have a basic sense of the ways you can make money. Some revenue streams are simple to understand, like playing shows, or selling CDs or t-shirts. But there are many, many more ways that musicians can earn money from their compositions, performances, sound recordings, brand, or knowledge of the craft. We list 40 of them below.

SONGWRITER AND COMPOSER REVENUE

1. Publisher Advance: Bulk payment to songwriter/composer as part of a publishing deal. Paid to songwriter/composer by publishing company.

2. Mechanical Royalties: Royalties generated through the licensed reproduction of recordings of your songs — either physical or digital. Paid to songwriter/composer by publisher, label, or digital aggregator like CD Baby or Tunecore.

3. Commissions: Typically a request from an ensemble, presenter, orchestra or other entity for a composer to create an original work for them.

4. Public Performance (PRO) Royalties: Revenue generated when your songs are played on radio, TV, in clubs and restaurants. Paid to songwriter/composer/publisher by ASCAP/BMI/SESAC.

5. Composing Original Works for Broadcast: Typically a commercial request to compose an original jingle, soundtrack, score, or other musical work for a film, TV or cable show, or an ad agency. Paid to songwriter/composer by agency requesting the work.

6. Synch Licenses: Typically involves licensing an existing work for use in a movie, documentary, TV, video games, internet, or a commercial. Paid to songwriters/composers either via publisher or record label, or via a direct licensing deal with the licensee (movie studio, ad agency, etc) if you are self-published.

7. Sheet Music Sales: Revenue generated by the sale of songs/compositions as sheet music. Paid to songwriter/composer by publisher, or directly from purchasers if you are selling it on your website or at performances.

8. Ringtones Revenue: Generated from licensing your songs/compositions for use as ringtones. Paid to songwriter/composer via your publisher or label.

9. ASCAPLUS Awards Program: Awarded by ASCAP to writer members of any genre whose performances are primarily in venues outside of broadcast media.

10. Publisher Settlement: Payment from publishers to writers for litigation settlements.

PERFORMER AND RECORDING ARTIST REVENUE

11. Salary as Member of Orchestra or Ensemble: Income earned as a salaried member of an orchestra or ensemble.
12. Shows/Performance Fees: Revenue generated from playing in a live setting (for non-salaried players).

13. Record Label Advance: Paid to artist as part of signing a deal.

14. Record Label Support: Money from label for recording or tour support.

42 STREAMS OF MUSIC INCOME

15. Retail Sales: Revenue generated from selling physical music in retail stores, via mailorder, or online. Paid to artist/performer by your label, or services like CD Baby or Bandcamp that help musicians sell physical product.

16. Digital Sales: Revenue generated from selling music digitally/online. Paid to artist/performer by your label, or digital aggregators like CD Baby or Tunecore, or directly from fans via services like Bandcamp.

17. Sales at Shows: Revenue generated from selling recordings of music at shows/live performances. Paid to artist/performer directly by fans.

18. Interactive Service Payments: Revenue generated when your music is streamed on on-demand services (Rhapsody, Spotify, Rdio). Paid to performer by your label, or digital aggregator like CD Baby or Tunecore.

19. Digital Performance Royalties: Revenue generated when your sound recordings are played on internet radio, Sirius XM, Pandora. Paid to performers by SoundExchange.

20. AARC Royalties: Collected for digital recording of your songs, foreign private copying levies, and foreign record rental royalties, distributed to US artists by AARC.

21. Neighboring Rights Royalties: Collected for the foreign performance of your recordings.

22. AFM/Secondary Markets Fund: Paid to performers on recordings used in film, TV and other secondary uses by the Film Musicians' Secondary Markets Fund.

23. AFM/Sound Recording Special Payments: Paid to performers for the sales of recorded music by the Sound Recording Special Payments Fund.

24. AFTRA Contingent Scale: Payments paid to performers when a recording hits certain sales plateaus.

25. Label Settlements: Payments from labels to recording artists for litigation settlements (MP3.com, Limewire).

SESSION MUSICIAN REVENUE

26. Session Musician/Sideman Fees for Studio Work: Revenue paid to you for playing in a studio. Paid by label, producer or artist, depending on situation.
27. Session Musician/Sideman Fees for Live Work: Revenue paid to you for playing in a live setting. Paid by label, producer or artist, depending on situation.

28. AFM/AFTRA Payments: Payments from the AFM/AFTRA Intellectual Property Rights Distribution Fund, which distributes recording and performance royalties to non-featured artists.

KNOWLEDGE OF CRAFT: TEACHING AND PRODUCING

29. Music Teacher: Revenue generated from teaching your musical craft.
30. Producer: Money from producing another artists' work in the studio or in a live setting.

31. Honoraria or Speakers Fees

42 STREAMS OF MUSIC INCOME

BRAND-RELATED REVENUE

32. Merchandise Sales: Revenue generated from selling branded merchandise (t-shirts, hoodies, posters, etc.). Paid to artist/performer by fans.
33. Fan Club: Money directly from fans who are subscribing to your fan club.

34. YouTube Partner Program: Shared advertising revenue, paid to partners by YouTube.

35. Ad Revenue: Or other miscellaneous income from your website properties (click-thrus, commissions on Amazon sales, etc.)

36. Persona Licensing: Payments from a brand that is licensing your name or likeness (video games, comic books, etc).

37. Product Endorsements: Payments or free goods from a brand for you endorsing or using their product.

38. Acting: In television, movies, commercials.

FAN, CORPORATE AND FOUNDATION FUNDING

39. Fan Funding: Money directly from fans to support an upcoming recording project or tour (Kickstarter, Pledge Music, IndieGogo).
40. Sponsorship: Corporate support for a tour, or for your band/ensemble.

41. Grants: From foundations, state or federal agencies.

OTHER SOURCES OF REVENUE

42. Arts Administrator: Money paid to you specifically for managing the administrative aspects of a group that you are a member of.

As you read the list, remember that a song has two copyrights:

The musical composition, which includes the notes and lyrics, and the sound recording, which is the performance of a musical composition. So if you hear Patsy Cline singing "Crazy" which was written by Willie Nelson, Willie created the musical composition when he wrote down the notes and lyrics. Patsy created the sound recording when she performed Willie's song, and it was captured on tape.

As you browse the list, it's important to keep these distinctions in mind since there are many times when different parts of the creative team are paid differently.

Don't worry if it feels like too much to keep in your head at once — we get confused, too!

Just take a deep breath and dive back in.

Get more tips on our website:

www.Pumpitupmagazine.com
and follow us on social media:
@pumpitupmagazine

SUMMER GOALS

EAT CLEAN AND GET LEAN

Get fiber, vitamins, nutrients, and enzymes from fresh fruits and vegetables.

Eat lean protein and complex carbohydrates at every meal.

Eat breakfast every day, within an hour of getting up.

Drink 2 to 3 liters of water (about 13 8-ounce cups) every day

Eat six small meals a day.

@pumpitupmagazine

Fitness

Best Routine

MORNING - NOON - NIGHT ROUTINE

Day 01 JUMP ROPE - 5 REPS - 30 SEC

Day 02 LEG PRESS - 3 REPS - 15 SEC

Day 03 GENERAL PLANK - 20-30 SEC

Day 04 STABILITY BALL CRUNCH - 3 REPS - 30 SEC

Day 05 SQUAT- 3 REPS - 30 SEC

@pumpitupmagazine

Self-Love

To Do List

○ Be grateful for yourself	○ Drink more water	○ Take a stroll in nature	○ Eat your favorite treat	○ Go to bed early
○ Listen to favorite song	○ Eat healthy meals	○ Take a nice bubble bath	○ Cook your favorite meal	○ Practice yoga
○ Go on a solo date	○ Write a journal	○ Give yourself a facial	○ Practice gratitude	○ Go to the gym
○ Watch the sunrise	○ Read a book	○ Explore a new city	○ Watch your favorite movie	○ Hang with good friends
○ Get some sunlight	○ Start a new hobby	○ Buy yourself a flower	○ Organize your closet	○ Watch the sunset
○ Take a day off	○ Learn a new skill	○ Accept your mistakes	○ Wear the clothes you love	○ Thank yourself

SMOOTH JAZZ PIANIST YULIA
FROM RUSSIA WITH
A SIGN OF LOVE

SIGN OF
LOVE

YULIA'S SMOOTH JAZZ GEM INSPIRED BY
HER SOULMATE

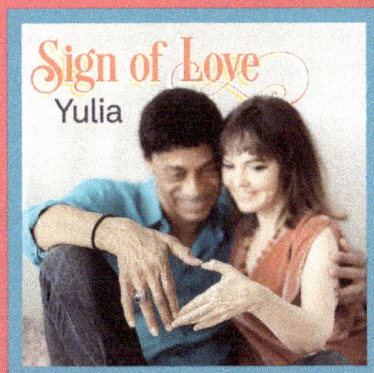

Spotify

WWW.IMYULIA.COM

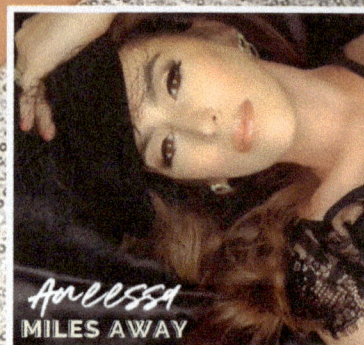

YOUR MUSIC CONSULTANT

"YOU BELIEVE, SO DO WE!"

We Can Help You To Grow Your Business

We are a monthly based service, we put faith in artists who has major potential, believed in them, and who are willing to spend their time and own money to work with us in building a successful music career!

Digital Marketing Services

SOCIAL MEDIA - STREAMING SERVICES - MUSIC DISTRIBUTION - PRESS RELEASE - PRESS DISTRIBUTION - PR

Radio Airplay and TV Commercial

TERRESTRIAL AND DIGITAL RADIO CAMPAIGN AL GENRES EXCEPT HEAVY METAL - CABLE TV AND MAJOR NETWORK COMMERCIAL

Licensing & Booking

CONCERTS, LIVE MUSIC, EVENTS, CLUB NIGHTS - RED CARPETS - FOREIGN LICENSING AND SUBOPUBLISHING

Why Choose Us ?

3 DECADES OF MUSIC BUSINESS EXPERIENCE
Platinium and Gold Records
MOTOWN RECORDS
UNIVERSAL
SONY
CAPITOL RECORDS

WE WORKED WITH:
Kanye West - Jay Z - Stevie Wonder - Michael Jackson - Germaine Jackson Smokey Robinson - Dionne Warwick - Cheryl Lynn - The Originals -

📞 **1 -818-514-0038**
(Ext. 1)
Monday - Friday / 9am to 6pm

FIND US :

www.YourMusicConsultant.com
30721 Russell Ranch Road Suite 140 Westlake Village, USA
Email : info@yourmusicconsultant.com

WEST END ORGANIX

Ageless Beauty, Organic Health

Look and feel younger and healthier with our natural remedies products!

www.WestEndOrganix.com

Discount: 10% off of your order - Code *WEO2021*

HOW CAN WE CELEBRATE
BLACK MUSIC MONTH

June is African American Music Appreciation Month! Created by President Jimmy Carter in 1979, this month celebrates the African American musical influences that comprise an essential part of our nation's treasured cultural heritage.
Formerly called National Black Music Month, this celebration of African American musical contributions is re-established annually by presidential proclamation.

STREAM YOUR FAVORITE AFRICAN-AMERICAN ARTISTS

One of the best ways to spend the month is by listening to and enjoying African-American music and giving it the hype it deserves. Explore new genres and singers, but also enjoy your old favorites. Streaming apps are also a great way to discover new artists.

TRADE PLAYLISTS WITH FAMILY AND FRIENDS

If you trade playlists with family and friends, you might be surprised by their favorite music listens. It's also a great way to get familiar with artists that haven't been on your radar.

READ UP ON AFRICAN-AMERICAN MUSIC HISTORY OR WATCH A DOCUMENTARY

To truly appreciate the different layers of this music, get into the mix by reading up on the history related to it. You will not only come to know all about the different moments and people that helped shape a genre but it will also help you appreciate the music you have access to today. Also, plenty of documentaries have been made on African-American music and the lives of the musicians. Find a title that interests you the most and settle in for a movie night.

DONATE TO A MUSIC SCHOOL

Many music schools teach African-American music. If you are interested in learning more about these genres of music, you can enroll yourself in a program. And if you can't find time for it, simply consider donating to one. There are also many African-American scholarships you can support that might be able to help someone follow their dreams in musical education.

VISIT MUSIC MUSEUMS

Another great way to learn about music history is taking a day to visit a museum. There are several museums across the nation that showcase music history. A few museums that I would recommend attending are the National Museum of African American Music (Nashville), GRAMMY Museum (Los Angeles), American Jazz Museum (Kansas City), Rock & Roll Hall of Fame (Cleveland), and Motown Museum (Detroit).

HOST A MUSIC GAME NIGHT

For fans who enjoy trivia, hosting a music game night with family and friends is a great way to test music knowledge and hear some classic tunes. Luckily, there are plenty of options between apps, cards, and board games. A couple of games I would recommend adding to your next game night is AuxGod: Hip Hop and R&B and House Party The Game.

WATCH INTERVIEW CONTENT - LISTEN TO PODCASTS
Thanks to different streaming, digital, and media platforms, fans have a lot of access to artist content. We recommend The Smiley J. Artist Zone Podcast!

The Smiley J ARTIST ZONE Podcast

CHIT CHAT AND MUSIC WITH BASSIST MITCHELL COLEMAN

1:29   -28:32

Listen to The Smiley J. Artist Zone

www.thesmileyjartistzone.podbean.com
and on all your favorite
streaming platforms!

BEST INDIE BLACK MUSIC ARTISTS

FREDA PAYNE "JUST TO BE WITH YOU"

Many people today tend to celebrate Valentine's Day because they feel that their loved ones need to be adored and appreciated at least on the 14th of every February. The majority of those will send flowers or other physical items that speak multitudes to the other significant half.
As we draw nigh to that time of the year again, the NAACP Image Awards nominated artist Freda Payne has added a drop of love through her soon-to-be-released single titled "Just To Be With You," which could be the perfect follow up soundtrack to your Valentine's gift.

"Just To Be With You" is a classical hit originally written by smooth Jazz sensation Aneessa and Motown producer Michael B. Sutton and performed by Aneessa. Primarily an asset belonging to Michael's "The Sound of LA" music label, the song has been re-cut and rearranged by the genius producer to befit the mellow voice of Freda Payne.
Featuring lyrics that stem from the deepest roots of Love,
Freda has done a solid towards making the track sound just as new and fresh as the original version.
Producer Michael B. Sutton continued to display his ingenuity as he redid the song with an astonishing feel of smooth Jazz.

This single is also currently available
on all digital platforms, through her website
https://www.fredapayne.com and on thesoundofla.com.

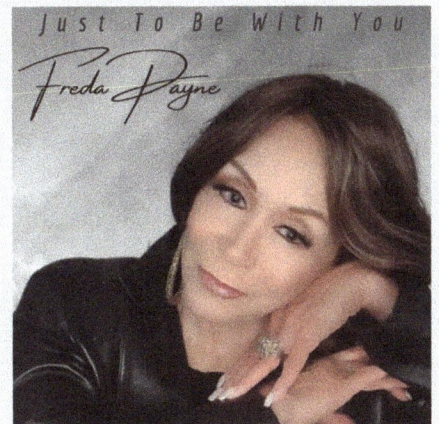

MICHAEL B. SUTTON "BAND AID FOR A BROKEN HEART"

C.E.O. at The Sound of L.A. and veteran Motown music producer MICHAEL B SUTTON has yet set out to begin this year with a crisp new sound that is about to mend all broken hearts. Thought of by many as one of the guides in the music industry, the LA-based singer and songwriter blends a sound of R&B and soul with his lyrical intimacy, attractive production, and organic rhythms on his new single
"Band Aid For A Broken Heart," *His new single invites us to be to be excited to be alive as we relive the feeling of being loved once again*
Download now on www.thesoundofla.com – on all digital platforms

"Band Aid For A Broken Heart" comes in with its elegant production and well-crafted lyrics written by Michael himself. The song speaks entirely about forgetting all that happened in the past and Michael B Sutton's mending your heart for the new has come. The prodigy promises an absolute healing for your pain that is about to last you till the end. While we learn to take the driver's seat in many occurrences in our lives, Michael's latest track brings a change of view around us that opens new paths and reminds you that you don't have to be alone through everything.

For over four decades in the music industry, Michael B Sutton has been well known for his personal nature, his honesty, integrity, professionalism, and attention to detail.
Having worked with some of the most celebrated acts of this century, including; Michael Jackson, Stevie Wonder, Thelma Houston, Diana Ross, Smokey Robinson, and more, Michael has proved to be one of the best producers and songwriters that has helped many artists on the way to stardom!

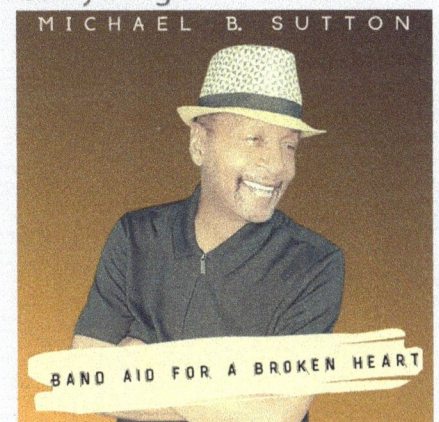

Buy Now

BAND of GOLD
A Memoir
FREDA PAYNE
WITH INTRODUCTION BY MARY WILSON OF THE SUPREMES
MARK BEGO

www.FredaPayne.com

amazon

"Don't be afraid to
follow your dreams."

UNSUNG HEROES

Since 1979, June has been designated Black Music Appreciation Month in the United States. Black musicians undoubtedly shaped the face of popular music, and to kick off the month, here's a tribute to five unsung African-American artists (or groups) in music history.

1. Rufus Payne, a.k.a. Tee Tot

Though not much is known about the life of Rufus Payne, he played an integral part in the development of country music, and therefore American popular music as a whole. As a street performer in Alabama during the '30s, known by the name Tee Tot, he taught an adolescent Hank Williams how to play guitar. Williams would of course go on to be one of the greatest country artists in history, thanks in no small part to the lessons he received from Payne.

2. Holland-Dozier-Holland

While the average music lover may not know the names Lamont Dozier, Brian Holland, and Eddie Holland, they certainly know the names of the people who have performed their songs: The Temptations, Marvin Gaye, and of course, the Supremes. Though Motown had a plethora of extremely talented performers, they wouldn't have been a success without any great songs to sing. If anyone can be credited with creating the Motown sound, it's the songwriting trio of Holland-Dozier-Holland.

3. Talking Heads' Backing Band

New wave pioneers Talking Heads formed in New York in 1975, and performed as a lean, punk-influenced quartet for its earliest tours. After the release of its fourth album Remain in Light, however, the band required an expanded line-up to go along with its dense, funk-influenced sonic palette. Five more members were added (a keyboardist, a guitarist, a percussionist, and two backing vocalists), all of which were supremely talented African-American musicians, and the band turned into a live powerhouse. The 1984 concert film Stop Making Sense perfectly captures this nine-piece at its most exciting.

4. Death

With Detroit's MC5 and Ann Arbor's the Stooges, there's an excellent case to be made for Michigan being the birthplace of punk rock. However, there's another band from the Great Lake State that was sadly forgotten for many years: Detroit's Death. Consisting of the three Hackney brothers, Death started off playing funk before switching over to a raw, protopunk style inspired by the Who. Unfortunately, the name "Death" made it difficult to secure a record deal, and the band split in 1976, remaining mostly forgotten until 2009, when seven of the band's songs were released as ...For the Whole World to See.

5. Willie Kizart

One of the defining characteristics of rock music is the distorted electric guitar, and the accidental creator of that distinctive sound was guitarist Willie Kizart of Ike Turner's Kings of Rhythm. According to legend, Kizart's guitar amp was damaged on the way to the recording studio in Memphis in 1951, which gave his guitar a gritty, distorted tone during the recording sessions for the song "Rocket 88," widely considered to be the first rock and roll single.

CELEBRATING UNSUNG HEROES FOR BLACK MUSIC MONTH ON WWW.KPIURADIO.COM
PUMP IT UP MAGAZINE OFFICIAL RADIO STATION

PHENOMENAL BASS PLAYER 𝄢:

Mitchell Coleman Jr

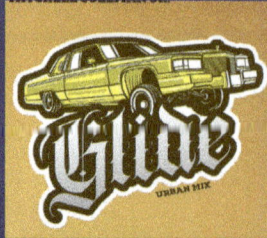

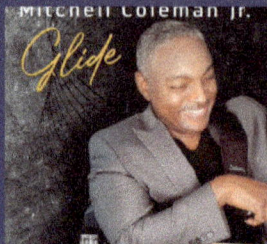

WWW.MITCHELLCOLEMANJR.COM

O.G. West Coast Collective Funk Therapy "Glides" Out with Healing Debut

As a pure and potent source of healing, you can never go wrong with Funk music. A very special collective of musicians, singers, writers and rappers emanating outta various subsets of Southern California has banded together under the moniker Funk Therapy to gift the world with some medicinal musical voodoo that soothes your mind while liberating your feet!

Introducing Funk Therapy, a wellness concept in West Coast groove, making its first house call as associates of bassist Mitchell Coleman, Jr. on the 'Urban Remix' of his latest single, "Glide." Coleman has already enjoyed success with two previous mixes of his cover of the intricate and innovative 1979 funk jam by the band Pleasure. Now, in collaboration who Funk Therapy, comes the most daring and different mix of all (available June 24 via The Sound of L.A. Records).

THE NEW ARRANGEMENT IS OUT OF THIS WORLD!

Producers Michael B. Sutton and Jason Anderson, in conjunction with Mitchell Coleman, Jr. and Funk Therapy, have slowed the music way down to kick a leaner, more spacey groove of drum machine and synths, a lead vocal sung through an old school vocoder plus the addition of an artful, thoughtful rap by Nigerian female mic checker Funanya.

The new arrangement is out of this world and guaranteed to introduce "Glide" to an even broader demographic of listeners, marinating in a vibration that is so old school, it's new again.

FUNK THERAPY IS THE BRAINCHILD OF LEGENDARY RECORD PRODUCER MICHAEL B. SUTTON

who took one look at all of the soul-crushing issues of the world today and decided that the remedy was some good old Funk Therapy. *"I've been in therapy over half my life,"* he says with a chuckle, *"so I am very aware of the importance of a sound and balanced mindset. Music has always been that thing for me, especially Funk. I play James Brown as much as I do James Cleveland (the Gospel legend) to keep my head straight. So, with Funk Therapy, we're debuting with our special mix of Mitchell Coleman Jr.'s hit single "Glide," a song that inspires people to move past their adversities, stay positive and keep on pushin'.* Later this summer, we'll drop a full EP – a mix of original songs and a couple of choice covers."

Funk Therapy consists of a revolving collective of musicians that, in its flagship addition, includes Michael B. Sutton, Jason Anderson, Hiroshi Upshur, Mitchell Coleman, JR., Josh Sklair, James Manning, James Gadson and Timbali Caldwell.

Once the full EP drops on August 26, lookout for live shows of their parliament patented process of full body "healin' with a feelin'!"

Pre save now: https://sndo.ffm.to/bjnqzox

Official website: www.funktherapymusic.com
www.thesoundofla.com
Record Label: www.thesoundofla.com
Follow Funk Therapy on social media:
https://www.facebook.com/funktherapy2/
https://www.instagram.com/funktherapy2/
https://www.youtube.com/channel/UCZOAvABvHG53wSX6AIpJ5e
https://soundcloud.com/funk-therapy-460149960

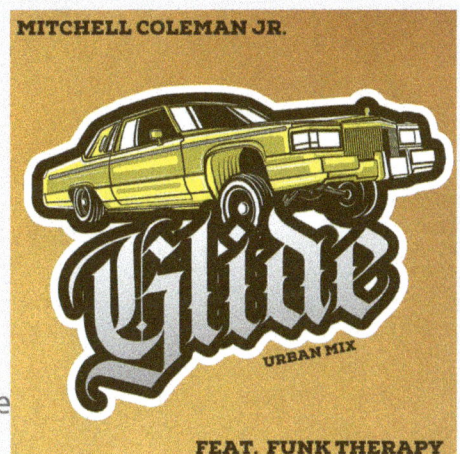

MITCHELL COLEMAN JR.

Glide

URBAN MIX

FEAT. FUNK THERAPY

PUZZLE #1

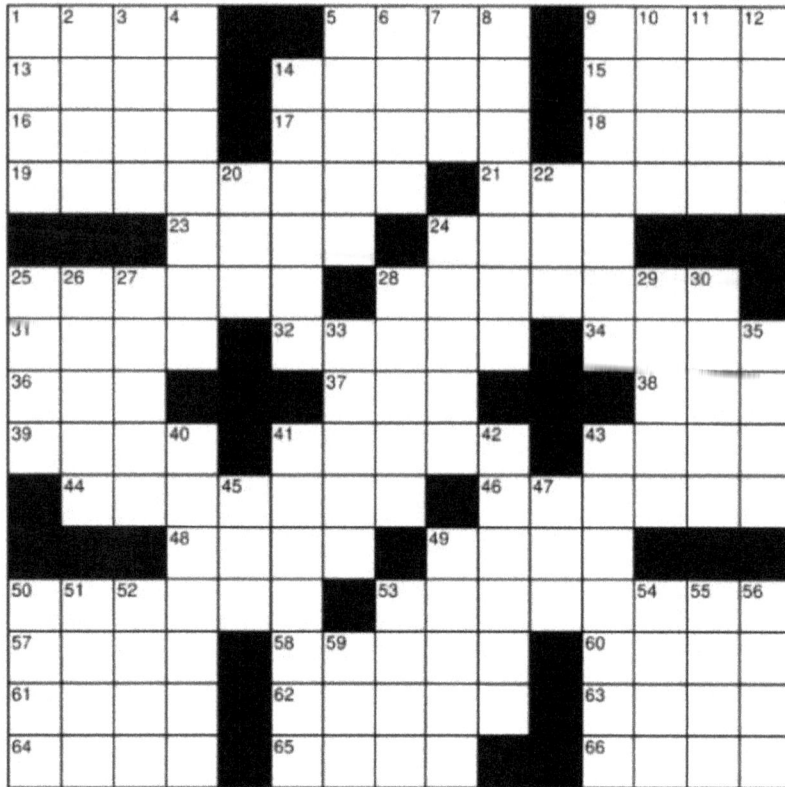

ACROSS

1 Space administration
5 Respiratory organ
9 Bivouac
13 Opaque gem
14 Forest god
15 Cruel
16 Land mass
17 Outline
18 Taboo
19 Aloft (2 wds.)
21 Dummy
23 Sand pile
24 Scent
25 Future
28 Can ___ (plr)
31 Was
32 Sing
34 First light
36 Paddle
37 Brooch
38 Day of the wk.
39 Writer Bombeck
41 Utilize
43 Pros opposites
44 Pistol (2 wds.)

46 Sticks
48 Momma
49 Cut into pieces
50 Tortilla rollup
53 Hold for foot
57 Native ruler
58 Use a car
60 Canal
61 What a clock tells
62 Helped
63 Incline
64 6th month (Jewish calendar)
65 Opp. of yeses
66 Hole

DOWN

1 Prophet who built the arc
2 Niche
3 Type of boat
4 Boy who finds magic lamp
5 Huge
6 Western state
7 New York City
8 Beowulf's foe

9 Put in the middle
10 Assure
11 Short
12 Cabal
14 Closefisted
20 Barbarian
22 Charged particle
24 Starts
25 Band instrument
26 Dreads
27 Italian physicist
28 Disgrace
29 City Boca ___
30 Moved back and forth
33 Musical production
35 Loch ___ monster
40 Suitor
41 Muslim holy month
42 Reverberated
43 Zeroes
45 Feed
47 Oodles
49 Inlets
50 Soft cheese from Greece
51 Among
52 The other half of Iwo
53 Bona ___
54 Spoken
55 Fancy car
56 Department (abbr.)
59 River (Spanish)

PUZZLE #2

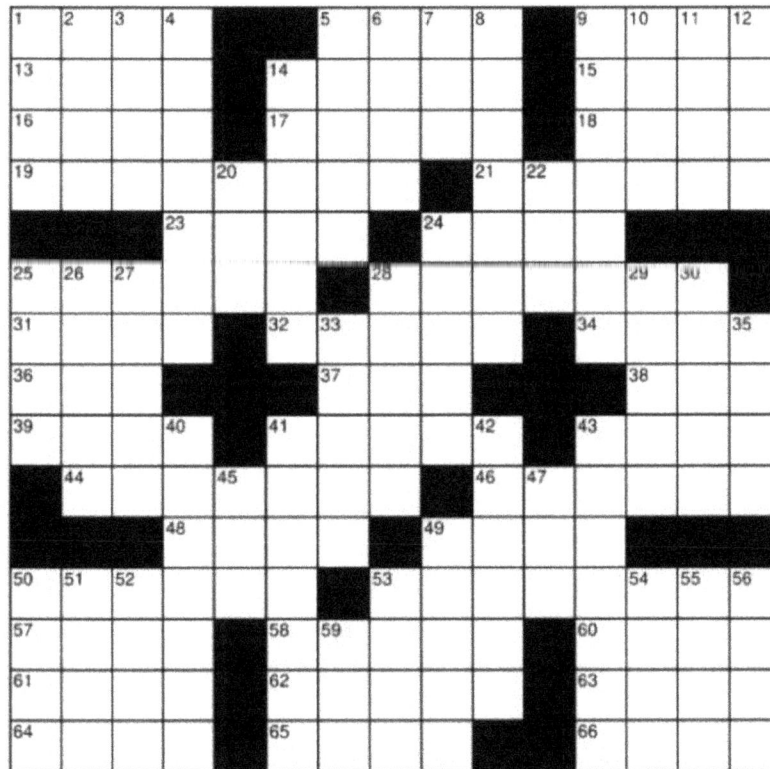

7 Clock time
8 Sate of being opaque
9 Rowers
10 Damson
11 Bullets
12 What dogs sit on
14 Calling
20 United Parcel Service
22 Paddle
24 Balancer
25 Feel the lack of
26 Beginning
27 Drug doers
28 Excuse
29 Boat locomotion needs
30 Unblinking
33 Opposite of ally
35 Upon
40 Greek muse of music
41 Rifle
42 Coaxing
43 State representative
45 Neither's partner
47 Nettle
49 Manhattan's neighbor
50 Crimp
51 Belief
52 Yacht
53 German "Mrs."
54 Brass
55 Black
56 Look for
59 Entire

ACROSS

1 Hook part
5 South of the border crazy
9 Opaque gem
13 Dunking cookies
14 Necklace fastener
15 __ matter
16 Clothing stitch
17 Artery
18 Hind end
19 _____ Eggs(Easter treats)
21 Universe
23 Imitated
24 Asian nation
25 Hair __
28 Female Performer
31 Institution (abbr.)
32 Type of race
34 Treaty organization
36 Compass point
37 Nada
38 Charged particle
39 Ecological communities
41 Renounce allegiance

43 Narrow opening
44 Giant wave
46 UN cultural branch
48 Italian boy's name
49 Cereal ingredient
50 Threads
53 Smaller than destroyer ships
57 Scent
58 Moses' brother
60 Hose
61 Bounce
62 Clank
63 Band instrument
64 Woo
65 Part of the "KKK"
66 Stink

DOWN

1 Pear type
2 Region
3 Looked at a book
4 Pompous language
5 Architect Frank __ Wright
6 Boat movers

SOLUTION #1

N	A	S	A		L	U	N	G		C	A	M	P
O	P	A	L		S	A	T	Y	R	E	V	I	L
A	S	I	A		T	R	A	C	E	N	O	N	O
H	E	L	D	H	I	G	H		N	I	T	W	I	T
			D	U	N	E		O	D	O	R		
O	F	F	I	N	G		O	P	E	N	E	R	S
B	E	E	N		Y	O	D	E	L	D	A	W	N
O	A	R			P	I	N			T	U	E	
E	R	M	A		R	E	U	S	E	C	O	N	S
	S	I	D	E	A	R	M		C	L	I	N	G	S
	M	A	M	A		C	H	O	P				
F	A	J	I	T	A		F	O	O	T	H	O	L	D
E	M	I	R		D	R	I	V	E	E	R	I	E
T	I	M	E		A	I	D	E	D	R	A	M	P
A	D	A	R		N	O	E	S		S	L	O	T

SOLUTION #2

B	A	R	B		L	O	C	O		O	P	A	L
O	R	E	O		C	L	A	S	P	A	L	M	A
S	E	A	M		A	O	R	T	A	R	U	M	P
C	A	D	B	U	R	Y	S		C	O	S	M	O	S
			A	P	E	D		S	I	A	M		
M	O	U	S	S	E		A	C	T	R	E	S	S
I	N	S	T		R	E	L	A	Y	N	A	T	O
S	S	E			N	I	L			I	O	N	
S	E	R	E		R	E	B	E	L	S	L	I	T
	T	S	U	N	A	M	I		U	N	E	S	C	O
	T	O	N	Y		B	R	A	N				
F	I	B	E	R	S		F	R	I	G	A	T	E	S
O	D	O	R		A	A	R	O	N	T	U	B	E
L	E	A	P		C	L	A	N	G	O	B	O	E
D	A	T	E		K	L	U	X		R	A	N	K

A Questlove Jawn

OFFICIAL SELECTION 2021
sundance
film festival

SUMMER OF SOUL

(...OR, WHEN THE REVOLUTION COULD NOT BE TELEVISED)

Pump it up
magazine

Tips For Taking Care Of Your
MENTAL HEALTH
C-PTSD & NARCISSISTIC ABUSE

People who have Narcissistic Personality Disorder have damaged self-esteem that is easily harmed by even small criticisms.
They are continually looking to shore up their weak areas of self-opinion.
To accomplish this need for self-preservation, they abuse and use other people, including, unfortunately, their own children, significant others etc..

Recognize the trait of the narcissist
A sense of uniqueness
Boastful behavior
Exaggeration of their talents
Grandiose fantasies
A sense of superiority
Self-centered behavior
Self-referential behavior
A deep need for attention and admiration

Recognize the trait of The covert narcissist
Passive Self-Importance
Blaming and Shaming
Creating Confusion
Procrastination and Disregard
(The covert narcissist is a professional at not acknowledging you at all.)
Giving With a Goal (to make themselves look good)
Emotionally Neglectful

How to Deal With a Narcissist
Set Boundaries
Avoid Taking It Personally
Advocate for Yourself
Create a Healthy Distance
Seek Help - Talk to a Therapist
Remove the Heart Wall
Emotion Codean energy healing technique for releasing trapped emotion

C-PTSD
Complex Post Traumatic Stress Disorder
is more severe if:
the traumatic events happened early in life
the trauma was caused by a wife/husband/parent
the person experienced the trauma for a long time
the person was alone during the trauma
there's still contact with the person responsible for the trauma

Symptoms of complex PTSD
Anxiety - Agoraphobia - Panic Attack
Alcoholism-Drug Abuse
Negative thoughts about
yourself, other people or the world
Hopelessness about the future
Memory problems,
Difficulty maintaining close relationships
Feeling detached from family and friends
Lack of interest in activities you once enjoyed
Difficulty experiencing positive emotions
Feeling emotionally numb

How to Treat complex PTSD
Set Boundaries
Avoid Taking It Personally
Advocate for Yourself
Create a Healthy Distance
Seek Help - Talk to a Therapist
Remove the Heart Wall
with the help of a Healer

@pumpitupmagazine
www.pumpitupmagazine.com

9 781088 051870